HAIKU GOD

Some Mindful Musings on God, Creation, and Other Things

by

Stacey L. Jacobs, DMin

FIRST EDITION

© 2025 by Stacey L. Jacobs. All rights reserved. Fair use of this material is allowable for critical reviews, articles, local church teaching, or academic purposes. Else, no part of this book in any form may be reproduced without the permission of Stacey L. Jacobs.

Graphe1968@gmail.com

CONTENTS

PREFACE 1
PURE EXISTENCE 2
ASEITY 4
NECESSITY 7
ETERNAL 9
INFINITE 11
IMMENSE 14
OMNIPOTENT 15
OMNISCIENT 18
IMMORTAL 20
IMMATERIAL 22
IMMUTABLE 25
INEFFABLE 27
IMPASSIBLE 30
LIGHT 32
LIFE 34
BEAUTY 37
MAJESTY 39
WISDOM 41
SIMPLICITY 44
UNITY 47
TRI-UNITY (TRINITY) 49

OMNIPRESENT	52
IMMANENT	54
TRANSCENDENT	56
SOVEREIGN	58
PERFECTION	60
LOVE	62
HOLY	65
TRUTH	68
JEALOUS	70
OMNIBENEVOLENT	72
JUSTICE	75
MERCY	78
WRATH	80
HUMANKIND	82
SIN	86
BIBLE	90
CHRIST	96
SALVATION	100
THE HOLY SPIRIT	105
THE CHURCH	108
ANGELS	115
DEMONS	119
END TIMES	123
ACKNOWLEDGEMENTS	131

When I remember You on my bed,
I meditate on You in the night watches.
— Psalm 63:6

PREFACE

I wrote this book to help people on their God-discovery journey. This book is in haiku format, a type of Japanese poetry. Haiku poetry has seventeen syllables in only three lines. The three haiku lines have five, seven, and then five syllables in each. This form of writing is a simple way to impart complex ideas. Haiku words are few, but can reveal deep concepts, even about God.

I am a Christian, but I have tried to objectively pen this work. Though not perfect nor exhaustive, this is a good starting point for most. God is the primary focus, and creation follows close behind. The relationship between God and creation is also seen here. Anyone who is searching for God should find some benefit in it. It is, of course, possible that my desired reach has most certainly exceeded my grasp. Yet, my great hope is that this work will bring light to those grasping for God. The journey to a given destination begins with just one step. Even if this work's light is small, I pray it helps you take that next step.

PURE EXISTENCE
God is pure being and pure act. God does not become. God simply is.

Why is there something
Instead of nothing at all?
There must be a cause.

The universe is.
It clearly has existence.
But not of itself.

Cosmos once was not.
Cosmos will one day be not.
It is running down.

The cosmos began.
Cosmos causes not cosmos.
There must be a cause.

The cosmos began
By cause immeasurable,
Beyond space and time.

HAIKU GOD

Caused means contingent.
Contingent means dependent.
It needs a causer.

The much greater cause
Of contingent entities
Is an uncaused cause.

Cause does not go back
Infinitely. An uncaused
First cause must exist.

An uncaused first cause
Exists purely of itself.
It causes all else.

God causes all else.
God is purely existent.
The Uncaused First Cause.

ASEITY
God is self-existent. God exists independently of all else.

To exist is to be.
Things exist in their being.
From where do things come?

Do things self-exist?
"Thingness" points to dependence.
Are there things uncaused?

Dependent people.
People are living beings.
But not of themselves.

Contingent people.
They can do wonderful things,
But not cause themselves.

Parents precede *us*.
Their parents preceded *them*.
Theirs preceded *them*.

Eternal parents?
Parents *ad infinitum*?
Out of the question.

HAIKU GOD

Infinite being
Is Independent being.
Uncaused existence.

Uncaused is First Cause.
First Cause is unlimited.
Simple existence.

Uncaused existence
Is Purely Self-existent.
Of itself, just *is*.

Pure Uncaused being
Is Self-existent being.
God's Aseity.

God shares not glory.
Yet, Christ shared glory with God
Before the world was.

Before the world was,
The Word was with, and was, God.
Christ's Aseity.

ASEITY

Pre-cosmos glory.
God's Aseity shows it.
Christ also shows it.

God created all.
The Spirit was also there,
In the beginning.

Who can know God's thoughts?
The Spirit knows all God's thoughts.
One Aseity.

HAIKU GOD

NECESSITY
God is the only necessary being. God needs none. All need God.

I am. Thus, I think.
But thoughts exist without me.
Thoughts do not need me.

The cosmos exists.
It was here before I was.
Cosmos needs not me.

The mind and cosmos.
One spectral; one physical.
Neither one needs me.

The mind and cosmos
Have not auto-existence.
They both need a cause.

Things exist sans me.
Things do not depend on me.
No integral me.

Things do not need you.
Mind and cosmos predate you.
No integral you.

NECESSITY

Things are dependent.
If a thing, then contingent.
Contingent is caused.

All things need a cause.
That cause cannot need a cause.
It causes all else.

God is Uncaused Cause.
Uncaused is independent,
Of necessity.

Necessary Cause?
This must be, or none would be.
Necessary God.

ETERNAL
God is timeless. God created and controls time. Time cannot bind God.

Things have origin.
Their origin is in time.
They are not timeless.

Things exist in time.
But if they exist in time,
They are not timeless.

No timeless humans.
We want to live forever,
Timeless forever.

Why live forever?
Does "forever" come from us?
Timeless thoughts from time?

For what do we look?
Freedom from the time prison?
Minds hoping for more.

ETERNAL

Forever hoping.
Minds seeing past time limits.
Thoughts transcending time.

No forever time.
Forever is timelessness.
Unlimited time.

Unlimited time
Is no real thing; time began
By an uncaused cause.

Uncaused Time Causer?
Yes. Else, there would be no *now*.
A Cause beyond time.

God is the First Cause.
As First Cause, God is *timeless*.
God is Eternal.

Christ: before all things.
All things exist by His might.
The Eternal Christ.

HAIKU GOD

INFINITE
God is pure limitless being. Nothing is able to limit God.

God is Pure Being.
He is the Uncaused First Cause.
God simply exists.

God's Pure Existence.
Difficult to comprehend
What does not begin.

Humans have a start.
The cosmos has a start, too.
They both have a Cause.

God is Uncaused Cause.
There is no start date for God.
God started all else.

The Uncaused Starter.
Nothing at all precedes God.
Being sans limits.

INFINITE

Unlimited God.
No boundaries to Being.
God is limitless.

The Limitless God.
Uncaused Ongoing Being.
The Infinite God.

Infinite Jesus?
Jesus shared glory with God
Before the world was.

Cosmos sans humans.
If no earth, then no humans.
No earth, no Jesus?

Jesus shared glory,
Even before the world was.
Pre-cosmos Jesus.

Pre-earth glory share?
One must *be* to share glory.
Christ before cosmos.

HAIKU GOD

The pre-cosmos Christ.
He existed before time.
He is Infinite.

IMMENSE
God is boundless being. Therefore, God is simply immeasurable.

Unlimited God.
His being is unending.
Infinite isness.

The God beyond time.
If timeless, then Eternal.
Non-temporal God.

Being sans limits.
Atoms limit; God has none.
God is beyond space.

Limitless Being.
The Alpha and Omega.
Ever-existing.

Unlimited God.
No beginning or ending.
The First and the Last.

No space-time limit.
God is immeasurable.
Thus, God is Immense.

HAIKU GOD

OMNIPOTENT
God has no limits outside Himself. God's power is without equal.

No limit in God.
The Unlimited First Cause.
Inexhaustible.

God can do all things
In accord with His nature.
And none can stop Him.

Unstoppable God.
He does whatever He wills.
And He wills the good.

The good-willing God.
He is Infinite essence.
Infinite goodness.

Infinite power
Is in infinite being.
God is Infinite.

The Infinite God.
He does not have *some* power.
God: all-powerful.

OMNIPOTENT

God of Pure Being.
No limit in being God.
Self-existent God.

God of all power.
No limit in doing good.
Omnipotent God.

Is Jesus Christ God?
God created the cosmos.
By Christ, all was made.

Christ Jesus is God?
God shares glory with no one.
Except with Jesus.

God created all.
Christ made the seen and unseen.
Jesus Christ is God.

Is the Spirit God?
No one knows the thoughts of God.
Except the Spirit.

HAIKU GOD

Only mind knows thoughts.
The Holy Spirit knows mind.
God's Infinite mind.

God is Infinite.
Infinite knows Infinite.
The Spirit is God.

OMNISCIENT
God is infinite in knowledge. God knows all that can really be known.

God is limitless.
Limitless means unbounded.
The Infinite God.

God is Eternal.
God exists before all time.
God of timelessness.

God has no atoms.
God is Immaterial.
God beyond all space.

God made all atoms.
God created time, as well.
Atoms made in time.

The Unbounded God.
He is beyond space and time.
God fashioned space-time.

HAIKU GOD

All things are from God.
Thus, all things are known by God.
God is Omniscient.

All time is from God.
Thus, God knows all time.
God is Omniscient.

God knows everything.
What is knowable *is* known.
The Omniscient God.

IMMORTAL
God does not age. God does not get tired. God always was, is, and will be.

Timeless existence.
No decay is possible.
No *time* for decay.

Spaceless existence.
No atoms, thus no decay.
No *place* for decay.

No timeless cosmos.
Cosmic things exist in time.
And they all decay.

Eternal monads?
Decaying Leibniz atoms
All come to an end.

Cosmic decaying.
No immortal things cosmic.
Finitude in all.

HAIKU GOD

Things celestial
Exist in space for a time.
Finite existence.

What then will endure?
Spaceless, timeless existence.
This is God alone.

The unbounded God.
God is beyond space and time.
God is Immortal.

The Infinite Christ
Shared pre-earth glory with God.
The Immortal Christ.

The Incarnate Christ.
A three-day grave held Him not.
The Immortal Christ.

IMMATERIAL
God created matter in space and time. God is not made of matter.

God in man's image?
What kind of "god" would that be?
Humans make all kinds.

"Arm, leg, leg, arm, head?"
Anthropological God?
Eternally flesh?

A "spirit father?"
He begets spirit offspring?
To fill up planets?

A "harsh taskmaster?"
He beats on the unruly?
Has he no mercy?

The "pliable god?"
A "heavenly grandfather"
Winking at mischief?

Fire-made golden calves?
"Behold your 'gods,' O' Israel!"
Bad metal meddling.

HAIKU GOD

Non-existent God?
"He is not made of matter.
He does not matter."

None of that is God.
God is not made of atoms.
God made the atoms.

Matter takes up space.
Matter is measurable.
But God is Immense.

God is Pure Being.
Nothing predates Pure Being.
God is before time.

No space and time God.
Space nor time can constrain God.
God is Infinite.

God is not matter.
Neither is God temporal.
What is God's nature?

IMMATERIAL

God is limitless.
God is Immaterial.
God is Pure Being.

HAIKU GOD

IMMUTABLE
God cannot change in being or essence. God is only always God.

Change occurs in time.
Timeless being does not change.
It remains the same.

Change occurs in space.
Spaceless being changes not.
Constant existence.

All time-bound things change.
Dependent time-bound cosmos.
Kept behind time's bars.

All space-bound things change.
No existing molecules
Maintain constancy.

Then what does not change?
Spaceless, timeless existence
Is always constant.

Constant existence.
This is the Unchanging God.
Immutable God.

IMMUTABLE

Unchanging Jesus?
Human change, yes; Divine, no.
He is Infinite.

Jesus is the same
Yesterday, now, forever.
Immutable Christ.

Unchanging Spirit?
Yes, since He is also God.
Unchanging Spirit.

HAIKU GOD

INEFFABLE
No words fully describe God's essence. All of God exceeds all of words.

The Infinite God.
Can "unlimited" be known?
Not completely known.

God's Immensity.
Immeasurable being.
Mere *apprehension*.

Immutable God.
Infinitely unchanging.
Who can comprehend?

God's Triunity.
One Essence, but Three Persons.
Indescribable?

The Immortal God.
Cosmos ends, but God endures.
How can God be known?

INEFFABLE

Now we know in part.
One day we will know in full.
When He changes us.

Words describe being.
But words always come up short
Regarding essence.

Mere descriptive words
Do not limit God's essence.
God is beyond words.

Yet, words will suffice
To know *some* things about God.
Even God used words.

No *comprehension*.
For God's isness, mere words fail.
Apprehension? Yes!

Finite words for God.
God is known, but not fully.
Ineffable God.

HAIKU GOD

Fully God and Man.
Christ is two "Whats" in one "Who."
Nothing else like Him.

The Word became flesh.
God with us; smitten He was.
A rejected Christ.

Jesus could be known.
Joseph's son? No. God the Son.
Ineffable Christ.

IMPASSIBLE
God has emotions, but not like humans. God has righteous emotions.

Mad about the good.
Feeling good about the bad.
Trite humanity.

Misfortunate you.
I rejoice in your downfall.
Fallen humankind.

Your life is thriving.
I celebrate your blessings.
If you give me some.

Cain offered to God.
He did not give God his best.
Sin was at the door.

Cain envied Abel.
Abel offered well to God.
And he died for it.

HAIKU GOD

God is not like us.
God has changeless emotions.
No fleeting feelings.

God has emotions.
He feels good about the good.
And bad about bad.

We should be like God.
Feel good for good, bad for bad.
His image in us.

The Unchanging God
Always feels good about good,
And bad about bad.

Unchanging feelings.
God's Impassability.
Changeless emotions.

LIGHT
God is moral light, not physical light. God made the physical light.

God is no photon.
Physical light is photons.
God made the photons.

God created light.
Electromagnetic rays
Allow eyes to see.

God is not photons.
Photons are measurable.
But God is Immense.

God is not photons.
Then what kind of light is God?
God is moral light.

Moral equals good.
Moral light shows moral right.
Moral right is good.

HAIKU GOD

We would all be blind
If God had not shown us right
By His moral light.

Jesus is the light.
He shines in immoral night
And leads us to God.

The light of the world.
Not photonic energy.
Jesus giving life.

Now behold the Lamb!
He lights a path in darkness
So we can be saved.

LIFE

God is the source of all life. In Him, we live, move, and have our being.

I was born in time.
I was born of my parents.
They were born of theirs.

Parents from parents.
Parents *ad infinitum*?
Who started parents?

Humans are time-bound.
We come *into* existence,
Not self-existence.

Humans are mortal.
We depend on a life source.
No self-sustenance.

Uncaused is non-born.
Uncaused is Self-existent.
Necessary God.

HAIKU GOD

God is Eternal.
Eternal is timelessness.
No birthday for God.

God is the Life Source.
God is the Author of Life.
No life without God.

The Author made us.
He made humans beautiful.
Human lives please Him.

Beautiful writing,
That is the human life form,
Pleases the Author.

The *imago dei*
In us, both life and being.
We share divine life.

In the Word was Life.
The Light shined in the darkness.
The Light was the Life.

LIFE

Jesus is the Light.
Darkness cannot overcome.
Light that gives us Life.

HAIKU GOD

BEAUTY
God is good. The good is pleasing. God is pleasing to all who seek Him.

Things are beautiful.
Eyes see pleasing existence.
Mere delights of sights?

Beautiful people.
Behold pleasure manifest!
Mere human sources?

Amazing cosmos.
Astral aesthetics amaze!
But they too began.

Is beauty needed?
To please is to meet a need.
God can meet all needs.

God can fulfill needs.
Is this the sum of beauty?
Mere pleasing? Not so.

BEAUTY

Beauty transcends sight.
Beauty also transcends need.
It speaks to the soul.

Essential beauty.
It is both perceived and known,
With no eyes or needs.

The Beauty of God.
Marvelous beyond all sight.
Admirable God.

No beauty in Him.
Our faces we hid from Him.
An ugly Jesus?

The Word became flesh.
By dwelling here, He pleased God.
Beautiful Jesus.

HAIKU GOD

MAJESTY
God is infinitely great. The greatness of God is without equal.

God of All Power.
He can do what He pleases.
And none can oppose.

God of Righteousness.
He does what pleases Himself.
He always does right.

God of All Blessing.
Every good and perfect gift
From the Light Father.

The God of All Love.
No one to perish He wants.
All to save He wants.

God of All Glory.
His praises shall never end.
He reigns forever.

God of All Mercy.
He forgives numberless sins.
Saves by grace through faith.

MAJESTY

None can surpass God.
He is exceedingly great.
The Majestic God.

HAIKU GOD

WISDOM
God alone knows the best means to the best end. Thus, we should trust in Him.

Study and study.
Much study tires the body.
And what do you learn?

Learning and learning.
The midnight oil burns and burns.
But do you get truth?

Besides, what is truth?
Correspondence to the real?
Pilate's mere question?

Truth is knowable.
To deny is to belie.
Denial *confirms*.

Wisdom comes from truth.
Knowing truth can gain wisdom.
But what is truth's source?

WISDOM

Truth is that which is.
Ultimate reality.
Truth is transcendent.

God is transcendent.
But God is also with us,
To give us the truth.

God is the Truth.
Pure Existence is all truth.
God is the Truth Source.

Omnipotent God.
No limit to God's power.
God can do all things.

God knows everything.
Nothing is unknown to God.
God is Omniscient.

Knowledge and power.
God knows all and can do all.
God knows the best way.

HAIKU GOD

God is true Wisdom.
The best means to the best end.
We should trust in Him.

All-wise Jesus Christ?
He is the way, life, and truth.
God is Truth. So, yes!

An all-wise Spirit?
He knows all the thoughts of God.
God knows all. So, yes!

SIMPLICITY

God is not made of atoms, but God is pure essence. God is simple.

Limitless being.
This is God in His essence.
Not bounded atoms.

Atoms are time-bound.
They come into existence.
But they do not last.

Atoms change in time.
Atoms change in location.
Atoms are finite.

Humans are atoms.
In God's image they are made.
But not God's essence.

God has no "thingness."
Things exist in space and time.
Things change in space-time.

God is unchanging.
Humans are ever-changing.
Merely mortal men.

HAIKU GOD

God is not mortal.
God is not made of atoms.
God does not have parts.

A body has parts.
But parts are made of atoms.
God is not atoms.

God is Pure Being.
Sheer non-physical Essence.
No timeless body.

So, what then is God?
Pure Existence with no parts.
God's Simple nature.

But Jesus had parts!
Jesus is God. God had parts!
The time-parted God!

Two-natured Jesus.
Christ is two "Whats" in one "Who."
Human and Divine.

SIMPLICITY

Human Christ, in time,
Did have parts: Immanuel.
But Divine? No parts.

HAIKU GOD

UNITY
God is pure infinite existence. God is one essential being.

God is Pure Being.
Pure Being is one essence.
God is One Essence.

Three "Who's" in one "What."
Three Persons in One Essence.
Unity in God.

No ill-logic here.
Three Persons in one Person
Is impossible.

God is only One.
No polytheistic God.
That is more than one.

God is One Being.
Many gods are not One God.
"Many" means idols.

Three Persons are God.
Father, Son, Holy Spirit.
God's Triunity.

UNITY

Jesus Christ is God.
Christ shared pre-cosmos glory
With God the Father.

The Father is God.
Christ and the Father are One.
They are One Essence.

The Spirit is God.
Spirit knows Infinite Mind.
He is One Essence.

God is One Essence.
God is not a committee.
God is One True God.

TRI-UNITY (TRINITY)
God is one essential being, forever extant in three persons.

Three "Who's" in one "What."
Three Persons in One Essence.
God's Tri-unity.

"Three Gods in One God?
Three Persons in One Person?
I am so confused!"

"How can three be one?
One person has one nature.
That makes much more sense."

"How can one be three?
We all know one equals one.
Who has failed at math?"

"From where did this come?
The Bible has not 'triune.'
Man-made 'trinity?'"

"What does Scripture say?
Is 'trinity' even there?
This is confusing!"

TRI-UNITY (TRINITY)

Is this "preacher's vain?"
Or "confusion trinity?"
That is what Prince said.

Would one ever think
Of such a thing apart from
The Holy Bible?

Look into the Word.
God created everything.
But so did the Word.

God created all.
In the beginning, He did.
But so did the Word.

But "Hear, O' Israel!"
"God alone is the One God."
Thus, there is One God.

One is only One.
One times one times one is One.
Who has passed math class?

Christ solves this problem.
"I and the Father are One."
Jesus spoke in truth.

HAIKU GOD

A good-works stoning?
"You, a man, call yourself 'God!'"
Killers *un*confused.

"I am God the Son.
The Scriptures say, 'Ye are gods.'
Why would you stone Me?"

"I am God the Son.
Believe My works that prove this."
That makes two Persons.

No confusion here.
The Spirit knows all God's mind.
The Spirit is God.

The Scriptures are clear.
There are three Persons called God.
Scripture does not lie.

Three are co-equal.
Father, Son, Holy Spirit.
God's Tri-unity.

OMNIPRESENT
God is unlimited essential being, thus everywhere present.

No limits in God.
God sees all and God knows all.
None hidden from Him.

God is beyond space.
No space place for His essence.
No atomic God.

God is beyond time.
No clocks count down His isness.
God: second to none.

Unlimited God?
Yes! No matter, no minutes.
All places, all times.

God sees everything?
Yes! No hiding place from Him.
His gaze everywhere.

No place He sees not?
The darkness is light to Him.
His all-seeing eyes.

HAIKU GOD

The limitless God.
No space-time limits at all.
Omnipresent God.

IMMANENT
God is ever-being in all space-time. God is everywhere near us.

Omnipresent God.
In all places and all time.
Nowhere God is not.

But how is God near?
Nearness is proximity.
God is in space-time?

Do not misperceive.
Do not hear what is not said.
Listen for the truth.

God is not atoms.
God is greater than atoms.
God is Pure Being.

Unlimited God.
Boundless knowledge and power.
God is everywhere.

The everywhere God.
God is Immaterial.
No atoms bind Him.

HAIKU GOD

The Eternal God.
Maker, not hostage, of time.
No time-captive God.

No shackles on God.
None keep His Essence from us.
God is near us all.

Equally near us.
His Being is unrestrained.
God is everywhere.

The always near God.
God exists throughout cosmos.
The Immanent God.

TRANSCENDENT
God created everything. God is greater than all of creation.

God is Infinite.
The creation is finite.
God is the greater.

God is Eternal.
The cosmos exists in time.
God is the greater.

God is Pure Being.
Human being is through God.
But God is greater.

God is Immortal.
Men want to live forever.
Ever-dying men.

Omnipotent God.
God is inexhaustible.
The cosmos runs down.

God-made atoms: seen.
God-made angels are unseen.
God: greater than both.

HAIKU GOD

God is over all.
There are levels to this thing.
God is top-level.

God is above all.
Not God's "rank," but God's Being.
The God of glory.

Creator God reigns.
God has no crown-weary head.
God rules everything.

God strong and mighty.
Who is the King of Glory?
The Transcendent God.

SOVEREIGN
God is self-existent and omnipotent. God controls everything.

Does one question God?
Where is the storehouse for snow?
Answer. If you know.

Will one question God?
God hung the earth on nothing.
Care to explain that?

Can God do better?
When do pots create potters?
Respect Potter-God.

Does God hear prayers?
The Immanent God hears all.
But who will hear God?

God is all-loving.
God desires that none perish.
Yet many doubt that.

God of all mercy.
Restraint that allows rescue
Of many who doubt.

HAIKU GOD

God should do better.
Why should suffering persist?
If God really loves?

Unwise questioning.
Creation reveals God's love.
But who receives it?

Who knows more than God?
No one. Then why question God
And never trust Him?

God is Omniscient.
God is Omnipotent, too.
God subject to us?

God answers to none.
God controls all creation.
God is Sovereign.

PERFECTION
God has no actual or potential defects within His being.

God is Pure Being.
Pure is having no defect.
Defect-free being.

What is pure is good.
What is pure is the standard.
God is the standard.

What standard is God?
The standard for existence.
All exist through Him.

Pure being for all?
No. Atoms can cease to be.
God is Eternal.

Time is not atoms.
There is no physical time.
Is time then perfect?

Time is a marker.
Time marks the atom's decay.
God does not decay.

HAIKU GOD

God is Immortal.
There is no decay in God.
No frailty in God.

What then is "perfect?"
From where does this "perfect" come?
Who can conceive such?

Thought transcends space-time.
It takes us into the realm
Of the ideal God.

Impeccable God.
No fault can be found in Him.
God of flawlessness.

Pure Being is God.
Flawlessness is God's essence.
God alone: Perfect.

LOVE

LOVE
God's infinite devotion to humankind is without parallel.

Infinite passion.
Not realized in the flesh.
No Cupid's arrow.

Copulative love.
Same bed for male and female.
Is this really love?

Spouses, both in love.
Male and female together.
In a half-neat bed?

Business suits come first,
Then swimsuits and birthday suits.
Carnal fulfillment.

Lover of people:
Putting their needs above yours,
When it is useful.

The lover of things.
The world is passing away.
And the lust of it.

HAIKU GOD

Is love mere desire?
Mere longing for finite things?
Not so with God's love.

Impassible God.
He desires not as humans.
God wants good for us.

God of all Wisdom.
Knows and wants the best for us.
Ever-caring God.

The God of all care.
God acts out of what God is.
The True God is Love.

God is Eternal.
God is Love. Eternal Love.
No temporal lust.

God's love will not fail.
God does not do *quid pro quo*.
God's love is a gift.

LOVE

God loves everyone.
No one is unlovable.
All are always loved.

Is love licentious?
Will God's love let sin slide by?
Absolutely not.

God's love forgives sin.
Giving one a chance to turn
From sin and to Him.

"I love God so much!"
If you love God, then serve God.
Not just when useful.

God's love does not force.
Forced love is nonsensical.
God's love sets us free.

The Son loves each one.
Any who trust in Jesus
Are set free indeed.

HAIKU GOD

HOLY
God is totally set apart from creation and God cannot sin.

People often sin.
Sin is not doing God's will.
To sin is human.

Human beings sin.
Sinning opposes God's will.
Immoral mortals.

"Can God commit sin?"
God cannot deny Himself.
No, God cannot sin.

Sin involves changing.
Sinless to sinful changing.
God is Unchanging.

God is not like us.
We just change, change, change, and change.
Then our time is up.

God is Immortal.
God eternally exists.
Ever-living God.

HOLY

God is not matter.
God created all matter.
And God does matter.

The Good God matters.
God alone reveals the good.
We should do the good.

Eternal goodness.
God's nature aptly described.
Infinite goodness.

Can God oppose God?
God is Immutably good.
No. Changeless goodness.

God overcomes sin.
Sin does not overcome God.
Sin affects not God.

Sin cannot touch God.
God is set apart from sin.
Sinless Holy God.

HAIKU GOD

"But sin touched Jesus!
Jesus is God. Sin touched God!
God is still Holy?"

Two-natured Jesus.
Christ is two "Whats" in one "Who."
Human and Divine.

Sin-touched Jesus Christ:
His death paid for all our sins.
But Divine? Sin-free.

TRUTH
God is Ultimate Reality. Thus, God is the Source of all truth.

It is what it is.
It will be what it will be.
It was what it was.

"True" is what it is.
The "truth" tells it like it is.
They are what they are.

Truth shows what is real.
Truth matches reality.
Untruth is a lie.

Red is only red.
Red is not non-red, but red.
Non-contradiction.

Excluded Middle.
Either A or something else.
Either this or not.

Inference in truth.
A is B and B is C.
Therefore, A is C.

HAIKU GOD

Either God or none.
If others than God, then false.
Mere idolatry.

God is the Truth Source.
Truth comes from, refers to, God.
Untruth obscures God.

God alone is God.
Idols are no gods at all.
Untruthful demons.

"Can God tell a lie?"
God is Immutable Truth.
No, God cannot lie.

"Human beings lie.
Human Jesus must have lied?"
No. He was God-Man.

JEALOUS
God does not desire material things, but defends His righteousness.

God desires no gold.
Silver or gold have we none
That satisfy God.

What if God hungered?
Would God really come to us?
God owns the cosmos.

Does God want a car?
No. God is Omnipresent.
All places, all times.

Does God want a house?
No. Houses are for mortals.
God is Immortal.

Does God want power?
No. God is Omnipotent.
God is All-Power.

HAIKU GOD

Fame. Does God want it?
God is known through what is made.
Cosmos speaks His Name.

Humans covet things.
God covets nothing at all.
Can God be jealous?

What is jealousy?
For humans, mere coveting
That which we have not.

Jealous zeal is bad.
Evil human hankering.
Unrighteous desire.

God is not like us.
God's zeal is for Holiness,
There is none like God.

God alone is God.
With great zeal, God guards this Truth.
Zealous, not jealous.

OMNIBENEVOLENT
God is good all the time. All the time, God is good. Eternal goodness.

I know what is bad.
But to know bad presumes good.
So, there must be good.

But what is the "bad?"
It is what is not helpful.
It is what destroys.

Then what is the "good?"
It is what helps us the most.
God helps us the most.

"Good" depends on me?
Is "bad" merely subjective?
Is there a standard?

God is the standard.
Timeless, Limitless Being.
God always just *is*.

HAIKU GOD

All-wise Creator.
Knows all the best things for us.
And desires our good.

God of all power.
Can do what is best for us.
And gives us the best.

God gives us the best.
Good is a part of the best.
God gives us the good.

We know what is good.
It is what helps us the most.
God gives us this help.

Can God give the good?
Is God the Source of the good?
Is God really good?

God created all.
He called it all "very good."
God does give the good.

OMNIBENEVOLENT

God's Limitless Love.
God always loves doing good.
God is the Good Source.

God always helps us.
God acts out of what He *is*.
God does, and *is*, Good.

HAIKU GOD

JUSTICE
God is holy and righteous. God gives each person what each one deserves.

God is always good.
God gives us what we deserve.
Because God is Just.

God gives good for good.
God does not play favorites.
God gives bad for bad.

God is truly Just.
God does not give bad for good.
That is injustice.

Truly Just is God.
God does not give good for bad.
Injustice that is.

Humans are unjust.
We sometimes give good for bad.
Crooked justice scales.

JUSTICE

Prejudiced people.
Often giving bad for good.
Unscrupulous scales.

Immoral mortals.
Sometimes withholding the good.
Scandal-ridden scales.

Justice pleases God.
If we do well, God is pleased.
If bad, then displeased.

Rewards are for good.
Obeying God is the good.
This is our life's sum.

Rebuke is for bad.
Bad ends in retribution.
Could be our life's end.

Giving what is owed.
Not just giving punishment.
But also rewards.

HAIKU GOD

God gives good or bad.
This is God's Justice to us.
Reward or rebuke.

MERCY
God's love lets Him withhold the retribution we are owed when we sin.

God of Holiness.
Sin cannot be near to God.
Nor is sin in God.

All sin is evil.
Real evil is in the world.
Real sin in the world.

But why is there sin?
Sin is disobeying God.
Not doing God's will.

Human beings sin.
Humans have contempt for God.
And will not obey.

God abhors all sin.
The Just God punishes sin.
That is sin's reward.

HAIKU GOD

But God loves us so!
He desires that none perish.
God wants to help us.

The great love of God
Does not give what sin deserves.
Love stays punishment.

In Justice, God's love
Supersedes sin's just reward.
This is God's Mercy.

WRATH
God will punish all sin. When mercy fails, God's retribution prevails.

God of all Mercy.
Takes no pleasure in our deaths.
God wants us to live.

Everlasting God.
Giving everlasting life
To all who believe.

What do they believe?
That God is, that God rewards
Careful Christ-seekers.

Faith in Jesus Christ.
Savior Jesus is God's Son.
Salvation in Him.

Some say they believe.
They have forms of godliness.
But have no power.

HAIKU GOD

Others feign the faith.
They serve with lips, but not lives.
Phony faith in God.

But some believe not.
"There is no God," the fool says.
Rejection of God.

Many deny God.
They deny and disobey.
Many commit sin.

Mercy forgives sin.
God's Mercy is Infinite.
But we are finite.

God endures, not us.
No sin *ad infinitum*.
A price must be paid.

God will punish sin.
When Mercy fails, Wrath prevails.
God's anger at sin.

HUMANKIND
Anthropology studies humankind, which is made in God's image.

Mortal means finite.
All humans have an end date.
We live, then we die.

Temporal people.
Humans exist in space-time.
No eternal men.

Free moral agents.
Humans can choose other than.
Minds making choices.

Dependent people.
No self-existence for us.
Contingent beings.

Spirit and matter.
All humans composed of two.
Hylomorphism.

Male and female mate.
That way, they make replicas.
More "God-images."

HAIKU GOD

Humans are mortals.
No self-created mortals.
Humans need a Cause.

God made humankind.
Male and female God made them.
God's image in them.

It was the sixth day.
God scooped up dust from the ground.
And fashioned the man.

"More than two genders?"
God made two: male and female.
Unqualified truth.

"Why were people made?"
Human life glorifies God.
God's glory displayed.

"Do we have purpose?"
We propagate God's image.
When we procreate.

HUMANKIND

"What is our purpose?"
We spread God's authority.
We reign in His Name.

"What else do we do?"
We proclaim the Name of God.
Exalting God's Name.

"Do we ever rule?"
Yes. But never each other.
Earthly dominion.

"Does God have a plan?"
Everlasting life for all.
God wants us to live.

Red, brown, and yellow.
Black and white. Pigmentation.
Within human skin.

Hate for skin color.
Skin does not define essence.
Foolish hating hearts.

HAIKU GOD

God made humankind.
Genetic markers for skin
Within our first kin?

God created us.
Melanin in the genome
Of post-flood people?

"Was Ham really cursed?
Were Black slaves really Hamites?"
Bad Bible scholar.

There are no "races."
Humankind in all places.
Just one human race.

SIN

Sin is missing the moral mark, breaching moral limits set by God.

God set the standards.
God is Holy and righteous.
We should be like God.

Broken God-standards.
Free moral agents break them.
Disobeying God.

God of Righteousness.
Sees people's unrighteousness.
Humans miss the mark.

God has set limits.
Good limits to help us live.
Humans breach limits.

Human choice is real.
The choice: obey God or not.
If not God, then sin.

Sickness. Disease. Death.
Pain and suffering in life.
All result from sin.

HAIKU GOD

Stealing and killing.
Robbery and pillaging.
Vestiges of sin.

Human fellowship.
None is found where sin abounds.
Broken fellowship.

Unity with God.
Broken when we break God's laws.
Sin breaks unity.

Sin's motivation?
"The Devil made me do it?"
No. Sin is a choice.

God planted a tree,
In the midst of the Garden.
A tree for knowledge.

God planted a man,
A stewardship gardener.
God commanded him.

SIN

"Eating you shall eat."
"Sans the knowledge tree," God said.
"Eat of it and die."

God made a woman.
She was God's gift to the man.
The man needed help.

They both saw the tree.
"Eye candy" good for knowledge.
They took a death-bite.

"Eve ate the apple!"
This is not about *fruit* trees.
And Adam ate, too.

God's command: broken.
Death ensued. Two were cast out.
Original Sin.

Just one single rule.
Free moral agents flouted.
Death came upon them.

HAIKU GOD

Many rules came next.
Breaking one meant breaking all.
A holy sin trap.

Sin's visitation.
Three or four generations.
To those hating God.

The wages of sin.
Certain death. The gift of God?
Eternal Christ-life.

BIBLE
The Bible is the God-inspired, inerrant, and infallible Word.

All truth comes from God.
God knows all that can be known.
God is Omniscient.

We can know some truth.
Our mental machinations
Allow us to know.

Minds musing on God.
Our cognitive processes
Focused towards God.

God wants us to know
About Him. Self-disclosure
In what has been made.

More knowledge needed.
So, when God spoke, people wrote.
Instruments of God.

The Books of Moses.
God's Laws and Israel's freedom.
And God began all.

HAIKU GOD

Moses was a scribe,
Writing down God's commandments.
Words of life for all.

Other scribes wrote, too.
Many writers over time.
Capturing God's words.

God sent the prophets.
Messengers for the Most High,
Speaking Divine words.

God sent apostles.
Uttering what thus said God.
God's holy heralds.

The Word at the start.
The Word was with, and was, God.
Word and God: the same.

The inspired Bible.
This is God-breathed Word for us.
Word, straight from the Source.

BIBLE

The breathed-Word from God.
All of it equally breathed.
Plenary, inspired.

Verbally Inspired.
Humans penned what God wanted.
Not their record, God's.

"Other inspired books?
Were all of those words God-breathed?"
Most probably not.

"Other holy books?"
Set apart, sure. But from God?
Just test them for truth.

No error from God.
The Bible does come from God.
Error-free Bible.

Inerrant Bible.
The autographs, error-free.
Pure-form first records.

HAIKU GOD

"We have but copies?
How do we know they are right?"
Put them to the test.

"How are they tested?"
Compare writings for the truth.
It will set you free.

Thousands of copies.
No material errors.
Highly trustworthy.

"Is the Bible true?"
It corresponds to the real.
Thus, it must be true.

"Fairy tale Bible.
It is wrong about science.
Science is the truth."

The Bible *pre*scribes.
Science discovers, *de*scribes.
No sin remedy.

BIBLE

Biblical morals.
Science talks about *matter*,
Not *morality*.

Morals do matter,
Not like atomic matter,
But *godly* matters.

Biblical morals,
Not scientific morals.
God's "shall" and "shall not."

Dinosaur Bible?
"Terrible lizards" not there.
"A bad-science book?"

Did dinosaurs sin?
Did they "miss the moral mark?"
Logically absurd.

Infallible book.
The Word cannot be broken.
It tells the whole truth.

HAIKU GOD

God, humans, and sin.
The Bible's main focal points.
God saving our souls.

CHRIST
Jesus Christ is the Son of God and God the Son. Faith in Jesus saves.

Jesus is the Christ,
The Son of God and Savior.
Life is found in Him.

Savior Jesus Christ.
"Christ" means the "Anointed One."
Anointed Savior.

A large sin-debt owed.
No one was able to pay.
None except the Christ.

Jesus came to seek
And to save that which was lost.
His divine purpose.

Christ: the King of Kings.
No earthly throne He wanted.
He created Earth.

HAIKU GOD

A body prepared.
Virgin-born by God's Power.
The Incarnate Christ.

Was this Joseph's son?
No way. This is God the Son,
Called Immanuel.

Christ was born to die.
Shed blood: the price for our sins.
Life is in the blood.

Jesus: born to die.
A strange way to save the world.
Yet, it can be saved.

Accusers accused.
False charges about His sin.
No fault found in Him.

Whipped, beaten, and scorned.
Then cross-hung by criminals.
He uttered no words.

CHRIST

He spoke in due time.
"Father, forgive them!" He said.
Then, "*Tetelestai*!"

The crucified Christ.
Three days in a borrowed tomb.
Death could not hold Him.

"I lay down my life.
I will take it up again.
When I am ready."

For any who doubt:
"Recall my Galilee words!
I will rise again!"

If He rose, then Lord.
Else, liar or lunatic.
But He rose. Thus, Lord!

Jesus rose again.
Death for sin no longer reigns.
Faith in Jesus saves.

HAIKU GOD

If you hear His voice
Today, then accept His gift.
He can save you *now*.

In His Father's house
He made a place for us all
To dwell there with Him.

"If I should go there,
I will return to get you."
His future promise.

SALVATION
Humans sin against God. They are saved by grace through faith in Jesus Christ.

People commit sins.
They miss God's clear moral mark.
They cannot hit it.

People commit sins.
They do not walk God's set line.
They go beyond it.

Sin can lead to death.
When one strays, one also pays
The debt owed to God.

What is the debt owed?
Death is the debt-penalty
When one commits sin.

"Wow, God. That is harsh!
One little sin does us in?
Is there no mercy?"

HAIKU GOD

Yes, there is mercy.
Along with the "twin" called grace.
Inseparable.

Mercy was the key
That made grace available
So all could be saved.

But faith is the fuel
That makes such grace effective
Unto salvation.

If someone believes
Jesus is the Son of God,
That someone is saved.

Saved, by grace, through faith.
Calvary crucified Christ:
The sin-debt was paid.

Saved once and for all.
Eternal security.
Secured by the Christ.

SALVATION

Through one's saving faith,
Justification occurs.
No longer condemned.

Not mere will-power.
Dead in sins and trespasses
Was our earthly lot.

God wakes up our minds
To our pitiable plight,
Then offers a gift.

Accept or reject
Is everyone's decision.
No middle ground there.

A free moral choice.
God's love makes it possible.
But God will not force.

Salvation applied.
An offer to anyone
Willing to believe.

HAIKU GOD

One is always saved
Once one believes in Jesus.
No lost salvation.

Why the confusion?
It is about sanctified
Versus justified.

Always justified.
One-time faith seals it for us.
Saved once for all time.

There is a process
In time: Christ conformity.
Sanctification.

Saved once for all time,
But *sanctified* over time.
No confusion there.

"I am saved. Now what?"
God's plan manifest in you
As you grow in Christ.

SALVATION

Love Creator God
With all your heart, soul, mind, strength.
The greatest command.

Serve God and people.
In due season, blessings come.
Blessings while on Earth.

Love God and people.
In due season, God rewards.
Blessings while on Earth.

"Where does that love lead?"
An eternal home with God.
Where joy never ends.

HAIKU GOD

THE HOLY SPIRIT
The Holy Spirit is God. He teaches, helps, and guides Christ-followers.

Spirit of the Lord.
The Spirit of the Father.
The Spirit of God.

The Spirit of Christ.
Spirit of the Son of God.
The Spirit of Truth.

The Bible reveals
The Holy Spirit to us.
The Spirit is God.

One of Three Persons.
The Spirit is a Person.
Divine, not human.

Personality.
It distinguishes people.
Person-traits displayed.

THE HOLY SPIRIT

Thinking and knowing.
Feeling, acting, indwelling.
Holy Spirit traits.

Impersonal force
Cannot know. But the Spirit
Knows the thoughts of God.

Impersonal force
Does not feel. But the Spirit
Feels and can be grieved.

The Holy Spirit
Is no Halloween specter,
Not a sheeted ghost.

The Spirit teaches,
Gives gifts and hope, commissions,
Fills, commands, convicts.

The Spirit provides
Guidance and empowerment;
Our Intercessor.

HAIKU GOD

The Holy Spirit
Fellowships with us, making
Us one with the Lord.

THE CHURCH
The group of people who are saved by grace through faith in Jesus the Christ.

Is "church" the building?
No. "Church" is those who believe
In Jesus as Christ.

Believers in Christ.
Special purchased possessions.
The people of God.

Ingrafted branches.
Connected to the True Branch
Through faith in Jesus.

Worshippers of God.
Worshipping the way God wants:
In spirit and truth.

Those who are "called out."
Not exactly so, but they
Do have unity.

HAIKU GOD

The Christ-built building.
"On this rock I build my church."
Hell's gates prevail not.

Christ worked miracles.
Most well-known? Resurrection.
Christ rose; the Church rose.

Church grew as Rome ruled.
Gospel seeds sown; it flourished.
Fed by martyrs' blood.

Jerusalem birth.
The first believers in Christ.
The Church spread from there.

The Antioch Church.
The first so-called "Christians" there.
Moniker of scorn.

Two church foundations:
Prophets and Apostles. Christ?
The Chief Cornerstone.

THE CHURCH

Appointed by Christ.
"You are the lights of the world."
Lights in the darkness.

"Cities on a hill."
Seen far away by others.
In them, Christ is found.

"The salt of the earth."
Giving flavor, preserving;
Changing what they touch.

Christ's ambassadors.
Representing God's culture.
God's will on the Earth.

Disciples of Christ.
By our love for each other,
All know we are Christ's.

The Body of Christ.
One Body, many members.
Unified by faith.

HAIKU GOD

The servants of God.
Learning, living, and giving
The Gospel of Christ.

The Church at present
Should be living to serve God,
Not to serve itself.

Some from within it
Seek to draw others from God
To themselves, Paul said.

Ravenous wolves wait
To devour God's people
From inside, Paul said.

A "God's-people Feast."
Some Watchmen wait to devour.
Preachers who pilfer.

Lambs taken off course.
Some blind, become the main-course.
With blind guides, ditch-bound.

THE CHURCH

The Church currently
Appears somewhat powerless.
Unplugged from Jesus?

Many Church buildings,
But little Church influence.
Mere money mongers?

Some seek miracles.
"Signs and wonders build my faith."
Misguided pursuit.

Church entertainment.
The "worship experience."
Zeal without knowledge.

Ignoring God's Word.
Promoting witless worship.
Bible ignorance.

The Church of today
Is still sustained by Jesus.
Else, it would have failed.

HAIKU GOD

Some have "rapture hope,"
When Christ returns for the Church.
Some wish Christ would wait.

Some want future peace.
Not often found in this life.
And if found, fleeting.

"Peace I give to you,"
But not worldly peace. Christ gives
Everlasting peace.

Christ gives the Bride peace.
The Church is the Bride of Christ.
Christ died for the Church.

"If I go away,
I will come again for you."
A future promise.

Christ rose for the Church.
A three-day grave held Him not.
Christ keeps His promise.

THE CHURCH

The trumpet will sound.
The dead in Christ will be raised,
Then clothed with new life.

The Bride will be joined
With Christ; no more death or tears.
All will be made new.

HAIKU GOD

ANGELS
Angels are spirit-beings created by, and exist to serve, God.

Created in time.
Not eternal, not timebound.
Angels have no end.

Jesus Christ the Lord
Made the seen and the unseen,
Which includes angels.

God made the angels.
They are not dead people who
Got wings in Heaven.

Angels are spirits.
Divine beings, not human.
They have no atoms.

Physical angels.
A contradiction? No. They
Manifest in forms.

Angels have a will.
It was for or against God.
Their wills were tested.

ANGELS

Good angels serve God.
They passed the test of their wills.
They serve God always.

Angels can learn things.
They learn what God teaches them.
Angelic students.

Angels have rankings.
Some are higher than others.
But they all serve God.

Isaiah saw them
In the temple. With two wings
They flew; eyes covered.

Some angels have names.
Gabriel and Michael are two.
They are El's servants.

Michael, the fighter.
An archangel who defends
Those who serve the Lord.

HAIKU GOD

Gabriel, the herald
Who brought news of Yeshua
To virgin Mary.

Some have "entertained
Angels unaware." Unseen
Seraphs and cherubs.

Messengers of God.
Sent to give us living words
From the Living God.

Messenger angels.
They brought us the word of God,
Revealing God's will.

God's faithful servants.
Ministers doing God's will.
Helping those in need.

Faithful ministers.
Serving those who will be saved.
Protecting their lives.

ANGELS

Angels served Jesus
In the wilderness after
Satan tempted Him.

Angels commanded
To guard Jesus from all harm,
His feet not stone-hurt.

Witnesses of God.
Testifying of God's works
Done by Jesus Christ.

Angels with Jesus.
One day coming to gather
All of God's people.

HAIKU GOD

DEMONS
Demons are fallen angels. The will of demons is to oppose God and destroy people.

Jesus Christ the Lord
Created all the angels.
They were very good.

Very good nature.
Untried moral character.
Would they obey God?

Angels have a will.
It was for or against God.
God tested their will.

Good angels obeyed.
Fallen angels opposed God,
and are called demons.

Created in time.
Not eternal, not timebound.
Demons have no end.

DEMONS

Demons are devils.
But they are not "The Devil."
That is Satan's name.

Satan: demons' chief.
The "father of lies" leads them
Against God and man.

Demons have knowledge.
But they know very little.
They did not know Christ.

Satan is cunning.
Beware of his scheming wiles.
He does not know all.

Unknowing Satan.
"*If* you are the Christ," he said.
Did not know Jesus.

Demons have knowledge.
"It is not our time, Jesus!"
They know of their end.

HAIKU GOD

Satan has knowledge.
It is great, but limited.
He knows how to lie.

Deceitful liar.
The same lies; but different days.
Aware of his schemes.

Physical demons?
No. They do not have bodies.
Deprived of bodies.

Demons can possess
Willing people or those who
May be unaware.

Demons can possess
Some animals, but they may
Need God's permission.

Demons can possess
No Christian. The Christian is
The Temple of God.

DEMONS

Holy Spirit-led.
God's holy habitation.
No co-owned Christians.

Demons can oppress
Christians if Christians allow.
Reject their scheming.

Satan whispers lies.
Christian ears attuned to God
Will ignore those lies.

Demonic warfare.
Though Calvary-defeated,
They futilely fight.

Gloom-dungeon demons.
Some are Hell-captives right now.
Until Judgement Day.

Demon punishment
Awaits in Hell. Hell was made
For demons, not us.

HAIKU GOD

END TIMES
The study of how this current age will end and a new age begin.

What begins will end.
This current age began and
Will certainly end.

This current eon
Includes the earth, the heavens,
And finite beings.

Mortal men and all
Dependent things great and small
Will come to an end.

"Why comes this ending?"
God is Just. God gives to each
What each one deserves.

God rewards the good.
God punishes the evil.
Each what each deserves.

The immortal soul.
The body dies. The soul lives.
To face God's judgement.

END TIMES

Moral agents judged
For what they have done in life
Whether good or bad.

Accepting Jesus
Is good; no punishment there.
But rejection? Bad.

Accepting Christ? Life.
Rejecting Christ? Death. The choice?
Accept Christ and live.

Jesus Christ saves
Any who believe in Him
As God's only Son.

Some believe in Christ.
Many believe Christ is false.
The end-times will tell.

Some finite being
Will be renewed or restored
Via God's mercy.

HAIKU GOD

The Earth will be new.
The old Earth will pass away.
No more corruption.

The heavens renewed.
Not God's divine domicile,
But the cosmic ones.

Before new heavens,
Christ comes: loud shout, trumpet, and
The Archangel's voice.

The dead in Christ will
Rise first; those remaining will
Meet them in the air.

With Christ they will be
Always. No more death or tears.
Comfort in these words.

From God's abode will
Come the New Jerusalem,
From Heaven to Earth.

END TIMES

The City of God
Will be with human beings.
The Lord will dwell there.

The Lamb will be there.
No more sun, moon, or starlight.
The Lamb is its light.

Many views exist
About the end of all things,
When the Christ returns.

They concern judgement
Of the world, God's wrath via
The Tribulation.

They also concern
The rapture of the Church, the
Dead and the living.

The views have two parts
About the Church's rapture,
Christ's return for it.

HAIKU GOD

First: Christ returns when?
Pre-, middle-, or post- God's wrath?
Will the Church suffer?

Second: will Christ come
Pre- or post- His thousand-year
Reign and rule on earth?

Some people say this:
Not a millennial reign
or tribulation.

No thousand-year reign.
The Amillennial view.
Rapture, then the end.

No Tribulation.
No wrath of God on the earth.
Rapture, then the end.

Many views abound
About the end of all things,
At least six more views.

END TIMES

A Pre-wrath rapture,
Before Christ's thousand-year reign:
"Pre-Mil, Pre-Trib" view.

A Mid-wrath rapture,
Before Christ's thousand-year reign:
"Pre-Mil, Mid-Trib" view.

A Post-wrath rapture,
Before Christ's thousand-year reign.
"Pre-Mil, Post-Trib" view.

A Post-wrath rapture,
After Christ's thousand-year reign:
"Post-Mil, Post-Trib" view.

Partial church rapture,
"Pre-mil, Pre-trib" view; just for
"Spiritual" saints.

Prophecies fulfilled.
No thousand-year reign, no wrath.
The Preterist view.

HAIKU GOD

Why so many views?
Bible interpretations
Cause differences.

Still, most believe that
God is just and will judge all
At some point in time.

But questions remain.
Jesus has not yet returned
To rapture the Church.

Jesus cannot lie.
He will return for His Church.
The Rapture will come.

God did not appoint
The Church to suffer His wrath.
A Pre-wrath Rapture.

A second advent
Of Jesus on earth, no one
Knowing He was here?

END TIMES

Jesus will return
To earth a second time to
Reign a thousand years.

Pre-mil, Pre-wrath view
Seems most likely in Scripture.
Christ's Bride glorified.

ACKNOWLEDGEMENTS

Aquinas, Thomas. *Summa Theologica*. Benziger Bros. edition, translated by the Fathers of the English Dominican Province, 1947.

Bloesch, Donald G. *Essentials of Evangelical Theology, Vol. 1*. Peabody, MA: Prince Press, 1998.

Geisler, Norman L. and Ronald M. Brooks. *Come Let Us Reason*. Grand Rapids: Random House, 1996.

Geisler, Norman L. *Systematic Theology, Vol. 2*. Bloomington, MN: Bethany House Publishers, 2003.

_____. *Systematic Theology, Vol. 3*. Bloomington, MN: Bethany House Publishers, 2003.

_____. *Systematic Theology, Vol. 4*. Bloomington, MN: Bethany House Publishers, 2003.

Hodge, Charles. *Systematic Theology, Vol. 1*. Hendrickson Publishers, Inc., 1999.

Lightner, Robert. *The Last Days Handbook, revised and updated*. Nashville: Thomas Nelson Publishers, 1997.

ACKNOWLEDGEMENTS

Nagel, Thomas. *Mind and Cosmos. Why the Materialist Neo-Darwinian Conception of Nature Is Almost Certainly False.* New York: Oxford University Press. 2012.

www.ingramcontent.com/pod-product-compliance
Lightning Source LLC
Chambersburg PA
CBHW071119160426
43196CB00013B/2625